PLANET ANIMAL

Steve Parker

Miles Kelly
PUBLISHING

First published in 2004 by Miles Kelly Publishing Ltd
Bardfield Centre
Great Bardfield
Essex CM7 4SL

2 4 6 8 10 9 7 5 3 1

British Library Cataloguing-in-Publication Data
A catalogue record of this book is available from the British Library

ISBN 1-84236-454-5

Publishing Director Anne Marshall
Design Jo Brewer
Cover Design GardnerQuainton
Poster Artwork John Francis
Picture Research Liberty Newton
Production Estela Boulton
Research & Index Jane Parker

The publishers wish to thank Ted Smart
for the generous loan of his illustrations

Other artwork by Alan Male and Jim Chanel

All other images are from Miles Kelly Archives

Printed in China

Contents

Walk on the wild side

As you tread carefully through a tropical forest or stroll across a prairie grassland, you are unlikely to come upon a hundred or so animals all gathered together. It's even less likely that creatures of every different size, kind, pattern and hue would arrange themselves in a tight-knit crowd, to show off their best features just for you. However you can imagine exactly such an event, as you gaze at the amazing scenes in this book.

PLANET ANIMAL *is a global celebration of the living world in all its colour, variety and activity. Giraffes rub shoulders with hummingbirds. Crocodiles keep a beady eye on river dolphins. Butterflies flit past parachuting squirrels. Fierce big cats hold back from attacking their usual prey of antelopes, wild cattle and goats. Numerous kinds of creatures pose with their close cousins in family*

73 Slow loris
One of the many nocturnal (night-active) mammals in tropical forest branches, the loris is a cousin of lemurs and monkeys. And it moves very, very slowly indeed.

48 Collared forest falcon
A fearsome raptor (bird of prey), the falcon swoops through the tropical forest canopy.

133 Jaguar
South America's big cat is perfectly at home in tropical swamps and marshes.

279 Coypu
A rodent or gnawing mammal, related to rats and mice, the coypu swims expertly in warmer rivers and lakes.

6

339 European bee-eater
This colourful bird prefers grassland and open country. It really does eat bees, and wasps too!

318 Cockchafer
This bulky beetle seems too heavy to fly as it drones slowly through areas of temperate woodland.

456 Sungazer lizard
Spiky scales protect the sungazer, in a dry habitat where survival is as hard as the sun-baked rocks under its claw-toed feet.

518 Mirror carp
Rows of large, shiny mirror-like scales separated by scale-less skin identify this member of the carp group. It lives in temperate lakes and slow, weedy rivers.

groups, including owls, monkeys, frogs, toucans, cichlid fish and kingfishers. The eight main scenes depict major and contrasting wildlife habitats. They range from the teeming treetops of tropical rainforests and the busy waters of steamy swamps, to the airy branches of temperate woodlands and the harsh, cold rocks of the high mountains. Every illustration brings together creatures from around the world and is packed with movement, detail and surprise. For example, there's not just one kind of duck, tetra fish or parrot. There are dozens. And here they are, arranged so you can compare, contrast and appreciate them.

In each main habitat scene, no words spoil the view. Colour-coding and numbered keys towards the end of the book identify every species using outline drawings. However it's fun to play hide-and-seek or an animal guessing game before you consult the keys.

The two pages that follow each main scene look at its most important features and most fascinating creatures in greater depth. There is information on where the animals live, what they eat, their breeding habits and how they survive in the modern world. Or how, in some cases – and we must remind ourselves why – they face the terrible threat of extinction.

The world's richest habitat

A tropical rainforest is dark, damp and quiet, with few animals or plants. But this is only at ground level. About 50 m above in the treetops is the world's richest wildlife habitat (and sadly, the most threatened). It's a noisy, seething, teeming mass of activity. Birds flap, butterflies flit and monkeys leap through the upper branches where leaves, blossoms and fruits thrive in the sunlight. Up to half of all kinds or species of animals live here.

8 Aye-aye
The aye-aye is one of the world's weirdest and rarest animals. It's a type of lemur that lives in a few patches of dense rainforest on the island of Madagascar. It uses its huge bat-like ears to listen for wood-dwelling insects, its strong fang-like teeth to tear off the bark and its very long middle finger to poke out the grubs to eat, as it creeps through the trees at night.

26 Koala
Koala 'bears' are not bears but marsupials (pouched mammals) related to kangaroos and wombats. The koala lives in warm, damp forests and also in drier, open woodland in eastern Australia. It does almost nothing all day and night except sleep (about 18 hours) and munch eucalyptus leaves (6 hours). The koala does not even drink, getting all its moisture from its leafy food and the dew at dawn and dusk. In fact its name is a local Aboriginal term for 'no drink'. Koalas look cuddly but they can bite hard and scratch fiercely. They also pass on a skin disease to people which is similar to athlete's foot.

19 New Guinea birdwing butterfly
The world's biggest butterflies, the birdwings have wings almost the size of your hands. They live across Southeast Asia and north Australia. The brilliant shining colours of the males warn predators like birds that they taste horrible. The colours also attract females, which are mostly dark brown for camouflage.

35 Verreaux's sifaka
This large lemur from Madagascar feeds mainly on leaves and fruits. It only comes down to the ground to eat soil, probably to get extra minerals. Its thick, woolly coat is white – or brown, maroon or even black. The name 'sifaka' comes from its shrieking alarm call when a ground predator like a cat comes near. For an eagle or similar aerial hunter the sifaka makes a different noise like a stiff stick rattled along fence railings. Sifakas are rare because their forest home is being destroyed for farmland – and because they are considered very tasty to eat.

46 Turaco
Turacos like the green (page 8) and red-crested are African fruit-eaters. Only turacos have green colour in their feathers. In other birds the green is due to the way the feathers reflect light.

50 King vulture
King of the kill, this vulture chases away other scavengers when it finds a dead or dying animal like a tapir or peccary. Most of its vulture and condor relatives fly over open country and spot food by sight. In Central and South America the forest-dwelling king vulture sniffs out the scent of dead meat, and especially dead fish along the riverbanks. If it runs out of rotting carcasses it may kill small animals like monkeys or lizards. The amazing coloured flaps of skin on its head do not develop until the vulture is about three years old.

2 Spider monkey
No monkeys are more at home in the trees than the spider monkeys of South America. Their tails are prehensile – the tail can curl around and grip a branch like an extra hand or foot. The monkey can hang by its tail as it gathers fruits and seeds with its hands and feet. Or it can do the opposite and hang by one hand as its tail grasps food and passes it to the mouth. All types of spider monkeys are threatened by the cutting down of their forest homes.

56 Flying lemur
Also called the colugo, the flying lemur of Southeast Asia is neither a flier or a lemur. It is a cousin of shrews and hedgehogs and although it cannot truly fly, it is an expert glider. It swoops between trees on parachute-like flaps of skin stretched between its front legs, back legs and tail.

58 Margay
The margay lives in Central and South America. It spends most time in the branches, stalking and leaping on prey like squirrels, birds, opossums and small monkeys. It is one of the most beautiful smaller cats with a striped coat pattern that earned it the name *tigrillo*, 'little tiger'. Margays were almost killed off for their fur but are now protected by law.

17 Hyacinth macaw
The hyacinth macaw is one of the biggest members of the parrot family. It measures more than 90 cm from the tip of its huge, powerful, nutcracker beak to the end of its long, hyacinthine (purplish-blue) tail. These macaws live in the swamps and palm groves of the eastern Amazon region. They clamber slowly through the branches using the beak as a third leg as they search for fruits, seeds and nuts. Like most parrots they make loud, short, raucous squawks rather than pleasant bird song. They also grow to a ripe old age of 30 years or more, when captive or even wild.

31 Palm cockatoo
Several chops with a hand axe may not split open the hard-shelled seeds of certain palm trees. The palm cockatoo holds the seed with one foot, puts it at a precise angle in its beak, and cracks it open with ease. Unusually for a cockatoo, it eats grubs and worms as well as fruits and nuts.

largest
Birdwing butterflies have wings more than 25 cm across.

longest
Flying lemurs glide farther than any other mammals (except bats), over 120 m.

barest
The king vulture has more bare, featherless skin than any other bird.

scariest
Local people once killed aye-ayes whenever they could, believing they were dead people returned as evil spirits of darkness.

For a full key to animals see page 40.

11

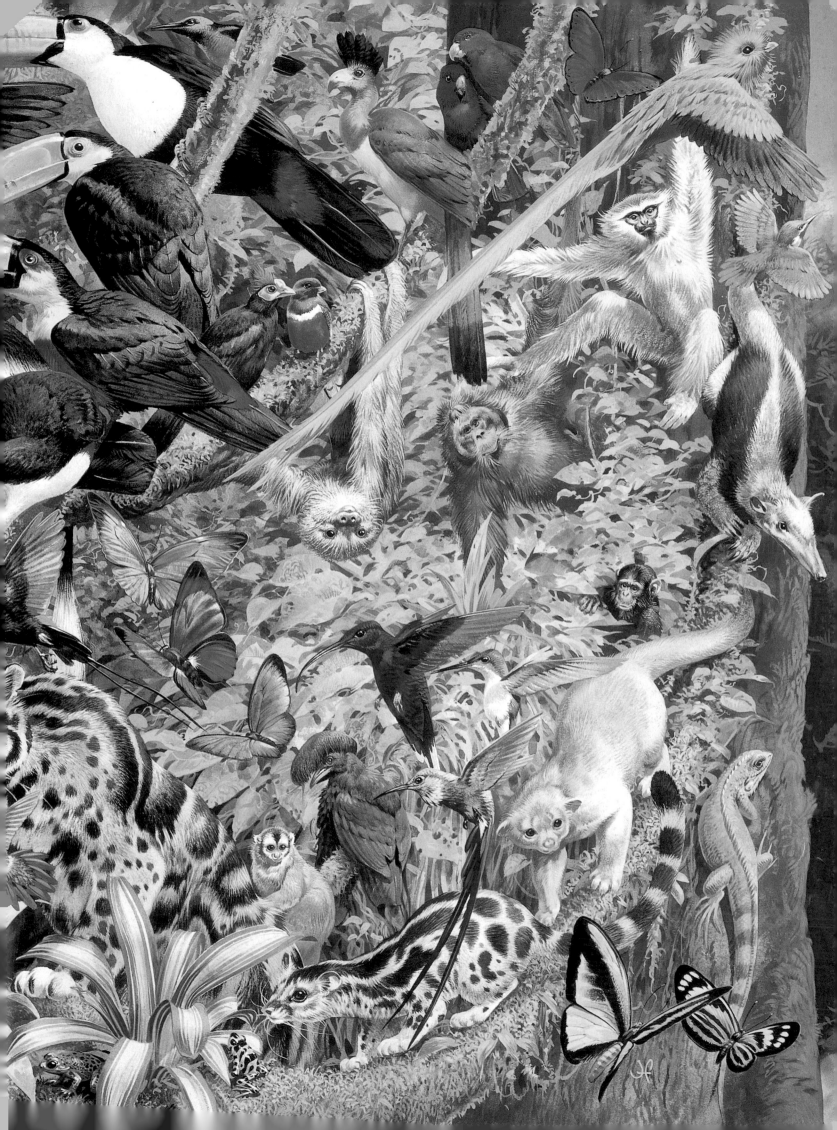

Leaping legs and grasping hands

Most tropical forest life is found in the canopy – the 'roof' of twigs, leaves, blossoms and fruits far above the ground. Some animals feed here but then climb down from the crowded tangle, to the understorey of lower boughs and trunks. Here they can travel more easily and also find quiet holes, branch forks and other places to rest and sleep. But they need strong limbs with grasping fingers or claws since a slip could still be fatal. Where an old tree has fallen, light streams through the canopy to the ground. Small plants spring up while vines and creepers dangle from the lower branches.

66 Green-billed toucan

The toucan's beak is nearly as big as the rest of the bird. Yet it is almost as light as a few feathers! It is made of a thin layer of horny substance (like our fingernails) over a spongy honeycomb of very lightweight bone. The beak's edges are slightly serrated (wavy-edged) to slice up larger fruits into pieces. For small seeds and berries the toucan delicately picks them off with amazing skill, tosses them into the air and gulp! swallows them whole. Toucans live in small groups that flap and screech all day as they forage through the branches for food.

128 Moon moth

There are many kinds or species of moon moths, named from the moon-like round or crescent markings on their wings. Each species varies greatly too, so moths from one forest look completely different from those of the same species but in a different forest.

109 Green iguana

Well disguised on a mossy tree trunk, the green iguana is active by day as it searches for fruits, shoots and other plant food. It grows more than 2 m long but over half is the whippy, tapering tail. This lizard is bright green when young but goes darker with age, especially the tail bands. It can race up a tree as fast as you run along the ground, its long clawed toes digging into the bark.

83 Tamandua (tree anteater)

The tamandua lives in Central and South America, climbing nimbly through the branches at night. When it finds the nest of some tree-dwelling ants or termites, it partly rips this open with its big front claws and licks up the insects with its long, sticky tongue. But it does not destroy the valuable food source. In a few weeks the ants repair the damage, build up their numbers – and are ready to be another meal!

121 Blue-legged tree frog

Blue is not the best colour for camouflage among branches and leaves. But the blue-legged tree frog is not concerned. Predators soon learn that its skin oozes a foul and poisonous liquid.

74 Chimpanzee

Chimps live in Africa, in bushland as well as forests. They spend most of the day searching for food like fruits, seeds, buds, shoots and soft bark. They also eat grubs, eggs and small animals like lizards. At night they sleep in tree nests. Sometimes male chimps get together in a gang and chase after another animal like a monkey or even a chimp from a nearby group. If they catch it they shriek loudly and jump about as they rip it to pieces.

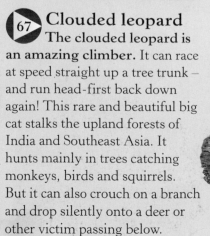

125 Golden tree frog

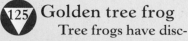

Tree frogs have disc-like pads on their toes which grip even the shiniest, wettest leaves. The golden tree frog eats very small prey like little moths, flies and baby slugs. Many tree frogs lay their jelly-covered eggs (spawn) in small pools of rain water. These collect in flowers or branch forks far above the ground. Insects like mosquitoes lay eggs here too, which hatch into water-living grubs. They are tasty food for the growing frog tadpoles.

94 Frilled coquette hummingbird

Hummingbirds are bird helicopters. They can hover in one place, go up and down and even fly backwards. Their wings flap so fast, 70 or 80 times each second, that they produce a buzzing sound.

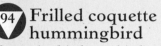

This fast flapping needs lots of energy which the hummingbird gets by sipping sweet, sticky nectar or honey from deep in flowers.

80 Emerald tree boa

Most boas are constrictors. They coil around a victim and squeeze it to death. Not the emerald tree boa. It coils its tail around a branch and then drapes the rest of its 1.2-m length through the leaves to look like a plant creeper. If a bird, squirrel or young monkey comes past the boa darts out its head and stabs it to death with its long, strong fangs.

111 Quetzal

Hardly any bird has tail feathers as fabulous as the quetzal's. The male grows them to impress the female at breeding time. They can be more than 60 cm long. This bird is a member of the trogon family from Mexico and Central America. The ancient Aztecs believed it was a sacred creature and a favourite of their feathered serpent god Quetzalcoatlus.

67 Clouded leopard

The clouded leopard is an amazing climber. It can race at speed straight up a tree trunk – and run head-first back down again! This rare and beautiful big cat stalks the upland forests of India and Southeast Asia. It hunts mainly in trees catching monkeys, birds and squirrels. But it can also crouch on a branch and drop silently onto a deer or other victim passing below.

smallest
The clouded leopard is the smallest big cat (the others are the tiger, lion, cheetah, jaguar, leopard and snow leopard).

noisiest
Toucans hardly stop squawking from dawn 'til dusk. Their calls are very harsh and sound as if the birds have sore throats!

cleverest
Some chimps learn to 'talk' using hand signs. They can tell you if they are hungry, thirsty, happy or angry!

For a full key to animals see page 41.

15

Jungle floor

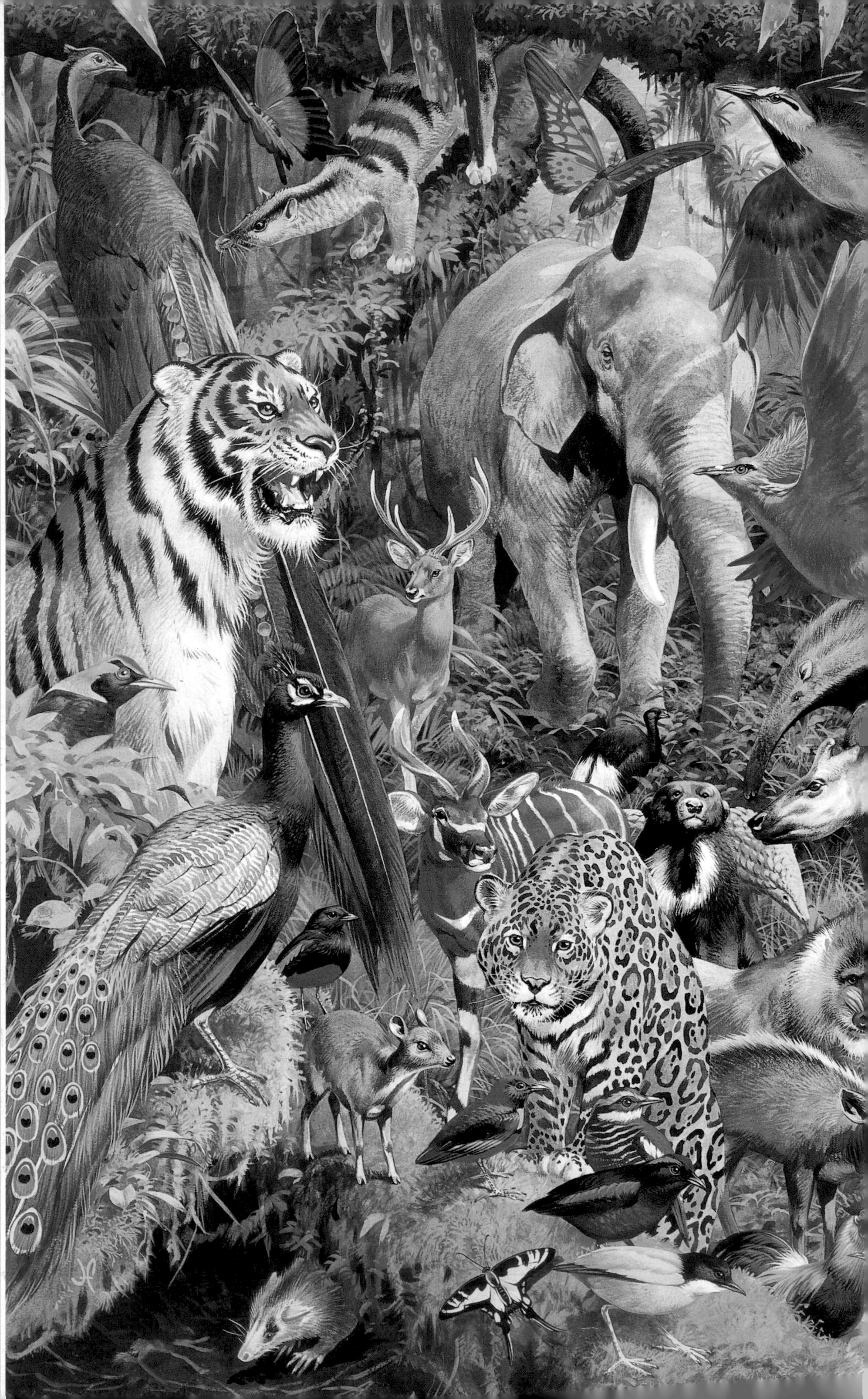

Trunks, horns, teeth and claws

The depths of the tropical forest are dim and quiet. But here and there big, shadowy shapes move slowly among the tree trunks. They sniff out leaves and fruits on the lowest branches and slowly munch their meal. Elephants, rhinos, tapirs, wild forest cattle and pigs are too heavy to climb! But they find plenty of food at ground level. If they are disturbed by a prowling big cat they quickly melt away as if by magic, into the gloomy undergrowth.

181 Lowland gorilla

The gorilla is the largest ape. A big male stands as tall as a person, 1.8 m, yet weighs three times more, 220 kg. Although powerful gorillas are peaceful plant-eaters. They feed in the morning and evening and sleep during midday and at night. The chief male of a troop may beat his chest, roar, thrash branches and even rush forwards, but only to protect the females and young from predators like leopards.

153 Javan rhinoceros

Javan rhinos are frighteningly rare – a species truly on the brink of extinction (dying out completely). At the end of the 20th century there were fewer than 100 of these huge but timid plant-eaters on the Southeast Asian island of Java. The biggest grow to a head-body length of 3 m and weigh 1.5 tonnes. They keep mainly to the forest interior and eat the leaves of bushes and low branches, occasionally taking fruits and pushing over young trees to get at their juicy buds and shoots. Unlike the African rhino, the Javan has just one horn. It lives alone unless it's a mother with her baby or calf. In the breeding season the males may fight each other, jabbing not with their horns but with their long, lower front teeth.

135 Tiger

The tiger is the biggest of the big cats, both feared and worshipped for thousands of years. There are several varieties in different regions across South and Southeast Asia. The Bengal tiger (above) from north-east India and Bangladesh is medium sized, up to 3 m from nose to tail. Tigers hunt alone, travelling up to 20 km each night in search of deer, wild cattle and pigs, and perhaps young elephants and rhinos. Very rarely a tiger gets a taste for human flesh.

169 Yellow duiker

Duikers look like deer but they are small cousins of sheep and goats. The yellow duiker lives in upland forests across the middle of Africa. It hides by day in dense bushes and comes out at night to eat leaves, fruits, berries, and also eggs and small animals like grubs and lizards. In turn it is hunted by leopards, jackals, big snakes and many other predators.

▽ 188 Drury's antymacnus butterfly

Flitting through the shady tropical forests of Central Africa, this butterfly is well camouflaged. It has a wing span of about 12 cm. Like most butterflies it has a tube-shaped mouth coiled up in a spiral under its head. When it lands on a flower it straightens the tube, or proboscis, and uses it like a drinking straw to sip the sweet nectar.

▽ 146 Great curassow

Strongly built, the great curassow is about 100 cm from beak-tip to the end of its tail. It lives in Central and South America. Although big and heavy, it moves very quietly among the branches as it finds a good roost (resting place) each evening. By day it creeps among the leaves and twigs on the forest floor, looking for fruits and berries. The male great curassow has a massive booming call to warn away other males and attract a female at breeding time. If a great curassow is caught very young it is easily tamed and makes a friendly pet. But once captive, it will not breed so taming them reduces their numbers in the wild.

○ 190 Jaguarundi

Also called the otter cat because it spends time in water, the jaguarundi is about the same size as a large pet cat. Its grey or rusty-coloured coat is plain not patterned, which is unusual for a wild cat. It's also an adaptable cat. Besides living in forests it can survive in scrub and even grassland. And it catches a huge variety of prey from mice, rats and rabbits to birds and their eggs, and water animals like fish and frogs.

▽ 138 Garnet pitta

Named after the brilliant red gemstone called garnet, the garnet pitta is found across Southeast Asia. It can fly but rarely does so. It walks about on the ground looking for worms, beetles, ants and other small creatures, as well as pecking at the occasional berry or seed. When in danger this pitta prefers to run off into a thick bush rather than fly away. If it has to take to the wing it does so in a sudden whirring flurry.

○ 144 Victoria crowned pigeon

There are more than 300 kinds of pigeons and doves around the world. The Victoria crowned pigeon is just about the biggest – around the size of a large farmyard chicken. Both male and female have the beautiful, delicate, lacy crown of head feathers. They eat seeds, fruits, berries and grubs.

▼ 131 Okapi

It looks like a combination of zebra and giraffe, it lives in the thickest rainforests of Central Africa, it's rare and shy… and its tongue is so long that the okapi can use it to lick its own eyes clean! This strange mammal is a cousin of the giraffe and can reach well over 2 m high to feed on leaves, fruits, shoots and buds. The mother okapi is pregnant for up to 15 months, one of the longest times for any animal except the elephant.

biggest
Tigers are the largest big cats. The Siberian tiger in the far east of China and Russia is 3.5 m from nose to tail.

strongest
The massive male lowland gorilla has the strength of three male humans.

rarest
The mountain gorilla is the rarest variety of gorilla.

newest
The okapi was the most recent big animal to be discovered by scientists, back in 1901. Unless there's another…

For a full key to animals see page 40.

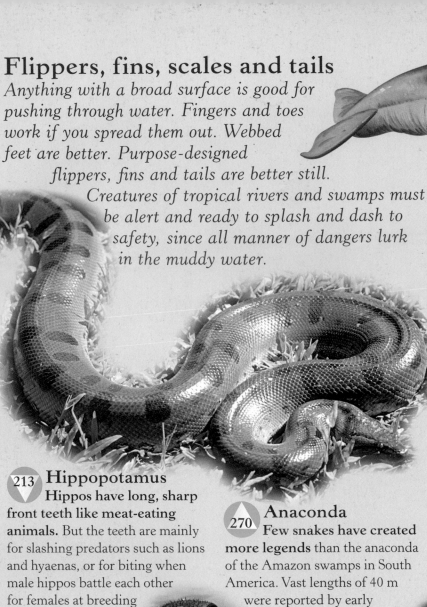

Flippers, fins, scales and tails

Anything with a broad surface is good for pushing through water. Fingers and toes work if you spread them out. Webbed feet are better. Purpose-designed flippers, fins and tails are better still. Creatures of tropical rivers and swamps must be alert and ready to splash and dash to safety, since all manner of dangers lurk in the muddy water.

213 Hippopotamus
Hippos have long, sharp front teeth like meat-eating animals. But the teeth are mainly for slashing predators such as lions and hyaenas, or for biting when male hippos battle each other for females at breeding time. The hippo is a plant-eater. It leaves its muddy pool at dusk to feed by night on bankside grass.

270 Anaconda
Few snakes have created more legends than the anaconda of the Amazon swamps in South America. Vast lengths of 40 m were reported by early explorers, partly because the size of a coiled-up snake or one lurking in water is difficult to judge. Up to 9 m is more realistic. The anaconda is not only the second-longest snake but is also amazingly muscular and powerful. Being a constrictor or squeezer, like the python, it can squash and swallow deer, pigs, tapirs or a 2-m alligator. The female does not lay eggs like many other snakes. She gives birth to as many as 45 fully-formed babies, each 60 cm long.

237 Sacred ibis
The sacred ibis was a holy bird in Ancient Egypt. It was so sacred that thousands were killed and turned into mummies, found regularly in tombs and temples. Today the sacred ibis is very rare in Egypt but it lives near water in other parts of Africa and across southern Asia. It jabs its beak into the mud for worms and shellfish. It also scavenges for leftovers in rubbish bins and on trash tips.

265 Amazon river dolphin
This dolphin hardly needs eyes because the Amazon and Orinoco rivers are too cloudy to see. So its eyes are tiny. Instead it finds its way by sound, like a bat. The dolphin makes underwater clicks and squeaks that bounce off nearby objects. It listens to the echoes and works out what is around. But the river today is so noisy with ships and boats that the dolphins have trouble finding food by this system, so they are becoming rare.

247 Night heron
The night or black-crowned heron is the most common and widespread of all herons, living in warmer parts of Europe, Africa, Asia and the Americas. It's about 50 cm tall and has two long, slim white feathers on the back of its head. The heron tilts these up when breeding to impress its mate. It hunts during twilight and darkness for fish and other water animals.

200 Indian forest kingfisher

Most of the 85 kinds of kingfishers have brilliant colours, like the Indian forest kingfisher on page 21 and the forest kingfisher below. They hunt by sitting still on a branch near the water, waiting for a small fish, frog or similar creature to swim past. Before you can blink the kingfisher has darted into the air and splash! dived onto its prey with its large, sword-shaped beak. This bird cannot swim well, especially under water. So if it misses its victim it quickly flaps away, back to its perch for another wait.

246 Flamingo

Largest of the five types of flamingo, at 1.2 m tall, is the greater flamingo. Most common is the lesser flamingo, about 100 cm tall. Both are called pink flamingoes yet they may not be pink at all, but white or grey. Their feather colour depends on the natural minerals in their meals of tiny worms, shrimps and other small animals and plants. The flamingo feeds by holding its head upside down, the dark end of its bent beak just under the water. It then 'dabbles' its beak and the comb-like flaps inside filter out the food.

197 Bichir

Bichirs are curious fish from Africa. They are 'living fossils' whose ancient cousins thrived more than 250 million years ago, even before the dinosaurs. Bichirs are about 40 cm long and hunt fish, frogs and similar aquatic animals in the weedy waters of lakes and slow rivers. In most fish the bag-like swim bladder inside the middle of the body is filled and emptied with gas bubbles, to help the fish swim up and down. A bichir uses its swim bladder like a lung to gulp air, if its lake is in danger of drying out.

194 Crocodile

The Nile crocodile of Africa grows to 6 m long and is a powerful and fearsome beast. It basks in the sun by day and lazes in the water at night, waiting for prey to come near. It even swallows stones on purpose to make its body heavier. This means it can float almost under the surface, with just its nostrils above to breathe and smell, and its eyes to keep watch. It catches any animal that comes to the water's edge, even a full-grown zebra.

206 Arapaima

The arapaima is also known as the pirarucu and by several other local names, in its swampy home of tropical South America. Like the bichir above it can 'breathe' by gulping air into its swim bladder. But it also has a bigger claim to fame as one of the largest freshwater fish in the world. It grows more than 3 m long and its vast mouth can swallow a 50-cm fish whole. It can do the same to a wild pig, a big snake or even a caiman (South American crocodile). However it usually feeds on smaller items like worms and shellfish. The arapaima is also caring parent (for a fish). It guards its eggs and its babies when they hatch.

bulkiest 1
The anaconda is the world's heaviest snake, at more than 200 kg.

bulkiest 2
Hippos are the third heaviest land animals after the two types of elephants. A well-fed, fat hippo (is there any other kind?) can weigh more than 3 tonnes.

bulkiest 3
There are tales of arapaimas weighing more than 200 kg. But 100 kg is more likely. This is about as heavy as some kinds of giant catfish.

For a full key to animals see page 41.

Fliers, gliders and jumpers

Temperate lands have warm summers but chilly, even cold winters. There are two main types of woodland. Deciduous trees lose their leaves in autumn. Evergreen conifers like firs, pines and cedars keep their hard, needle leaves all year. In warmer months many creatures fly, swoop or leap among the branches of deciduous trees, eating the soft leaves, fruits and seeds or the animals that live there. In winter they take to the woodland floor or move to still-green conifers for shelter and safety.

283 Red squirrel

With its rusty red fur and tufted ears, the red (Eurasian) squirrel looks quite different from its grey (American) cousin. Its main foods are seeds and bark of conifer trees and also fruits, berries and fungi. In Britain red squirrels used to live in deciduous woods. However the larger, stronger grey squirrel has taken over most of these.

326 Eagle owl

Massive and muscular, the eagle owl is the largest of all the owls. It is so powerful that it hunts other birds of prey like the goshawk (above), buzzards and falcons, and also other owls such as the tawny and long-eared owls. Under cover of darkness it even snatches young eagles from their nests, as well as swooping on chickens, grouse, rats, rabbits, hares and the occasional young badger or deer. Eagle owls were once widespread across Europe, North Africa and Asia. They even perched on the great ancient pyramids of Egypt. Now they live mainly in remote forests and rocky hills far away from towns and farmland.

289 Goshawk

Birds that soar over open country have long, broad, straight wings. Woodland predators like the goshawk have shorter, slightly swept-back wings which are the best shape for twisting and turning among the trees. Female goshawks are about 60 cm from beak to tail, males slightly smaller. They catch many kinds of prey up to the size of hares and pheasants, diving to stab them with their fierce talons (claws) and then feeding at leisure on the ground.

304 Monarch butterfly

Monarchs are champion insect migrants. They spend winter in the southern USA and Mexico, in vast roosts of millions which attract tourists. In spring they fly north, breeding as they go, for summer in the northern USA and Canada. In autumn their offspring fly back south.

314 Cardinal

With its bright red-pink feathers, head crest, black face and red beak, the male cardinal looks like no other bird. The female is similar but has a browner body. She builds the nest in a thick bush and sits on the eggs, then both parents feed the three or four chicks. Cardinals thrive in parks and gardens as well as natural woodlands in North America. They also have a wide variety of calls and songs which they make at any time of day and year.

312 Long-eared bat

This bat has ears four times the size of its face. They swivel and tilt to hear the returning echoes of the ultrasonic (very high-pitched) clicks and squeaks that the bat makes as it flies. This sound-radar or sonar system is how the creature finds its way and prey even in complete darkness. Such massive ears are needed because the long-eared bat, which has a wing span of 25 cm, lives mainly in woods. Its sonar must identify even small twigs and leaves, so it can dodge these as it swoops. (Bats of open country have smaller ears.) The long-eared bat can even hover above a leaf to snatch a beetle, moth or caterpillar – all done by sound.

292 Purple emperor butterfly

In summer the male purple emperor flits around the tops of oak trees. He darts at rival males to chase them away and then flashes his brilliant wings in the sun to attract a female. She lacks the purple sheen but her brown wings have the same white patterns and eye spots.

335 Golden oriole

These orioles have spread from woodlands into orchards and parks. They can be a pest since they peck apples and other fruits, not only to eat them but also to grab the grubs, maggots and other insects feeding there. Golden orioles spend summer in northern areas of Europe and Asia, then fly south to winter in Africa and southern Asia.

288 Red panda

The red or lesser panda is not nearly as famous as its 'giant' black-and-white cousin. But it eats similar food – bamboo shoots and leaves. It also munches fruits and seeds and hunts for mice, voles and small birds. The red panda feeds on the ground or in the lower branches at night. By day it sleeps on a comfortable branch, bushy tail curled around its head and body. Red pandas are found in the northern parts of Southeast Asia. The panda's head and body are about 60 cm long, the tail 45 cm. Although these pandas are not as frighteningly scarce as giant pandas, their numbers have fallen as their forest homes are destroyed.

319 Stag beetle

Don't worry too much about the bite from a male stag beetle. Its outsized 'jaws' are so big and heavy that their small muscles can hardly move them. This beetle grows up to 7 cm long, almost one-third being the huge mouthparts that look like the antlers of a stag (male deer). They are mainly for threatening other males and grappling with them at breeding time, in order to win the battle and mate with a female. Her jaws, on the other hand, are smaller than the male's and move more powerfully. She can give a painful nip.

337 Canadian porcupine

Can the porcupine shoot its long spines across a forest clearing at an enemy? No. But the spines or quills are very sharp and stiff. If the porcupine is threatened it rattles them and then rushes at the attacker, swinging around so the quills stab into its body. But this is only a last resort. Normally the porcupine spends its days sleeping in the fork of a tree, and its nights chewing buds, shoots and soft bark.

farthest
Some swarms of monarchs fly a yearly round migration or journey of more than 6000 km.

biggest
The eagle owl is the largest owl, about 70 cm from beak to tail-end and with wings more than 100 cm across.

yukkiest
Various butterflies drink at muddy pools to get extra minerals from the soil. Purple emperors have a different method. They suck up the smelly juices from rotting animal bodies and from squishy, runny animal droppings.

For a full key to animals see page 42.

Heat and drought on the plains

Where the climate is too dry for trees, but too moist for a desert, the land is cloaked with waving grasses. These plants are rich food for an amazing variety of animals. But grasslands pose a problem because, unlike a forest, there are few places to hide. So grass-eaters are usually very large, or very fast, or both, as defence against predators. They must also endure long hot summers, months without rain and the occasional bushfire.

420 Jackson's chameleon

This African lizard is green and white – at least for now. It blends in with the bushy leaves all around it. Like other chameleons, Jackson's can change its colour and pattern over a minute or two and become yellow, red, brown, grey or even blue. The excellent camouflage means flies, beetles and other small prey do not notice the chameleon until – zap! Its long tongue flashes out and grabs them on its sticky tip.

409 Bishop's weaver bird

Weaver birds are named because they thread together grass stems, small vines and thin twigs, twisting them in and out to create a large, strong nest. The red bishop or bishop's weaver is one of the most numerous, forming vast flocks that fly like clouds across the African grassland. They sometimes damage farm crops. The male is red and black only in the breeding season. Out of it, he is brownish like the female.

365 African elephant

The male African elephant or 'tusker' is the world's biggest land animal. Its head and body are 7.5 m long and the trunk and tail add nearly 2 m at each end. The tusks are greatly oversized upper front teeth (incisors) which grow with age to 3 m or more in length. Females have them too but much smaller. An elephant herd consists of mid-aged females with their young and a few other helper females or 'aunts'. They are led by an older, experienced female or matriarch. Young males form bachelor groups. Old males wander alone.

384 Gila monster

Only two lizards have poisonous bites. One is the gila ('heeler') monster from dry scrub and semi-desert in the south-west of North America. The other is the Mexican beaded lizard. Both have rounded scales like small beads which are coloured to form bright patterns. The gila prowls at night after small animals like beetles, snails, mice, young birds and little lizards. By day it sleeps in a hole or under a rock.

369 Vervet monkey

The vervet is widespread across Africa wherever there are grasses and bushes, a few trees for escape, and a nearby lake or river for drinking water. Most monkeys (except the large baboons) stay in trees but the vervet is extremely adaptable. It can climb, run and swim very well and it eats a huge variety of foods. It mainly scrabbles on the ground for buds, fruits, roots and soft bark and also worms, grubs, mice and other small animals. It also shakes bushes hard, hoping bird eggs or chicks will fall out.

360 Bison

Huge and hulking, the male bison stands more than 2 m tall at the shoulder and weighs over 750 kg. Along with the wild yak from Central Asia it is the biggest of wild cattle. American bison (not 'buffalo' as they are sometimes called) once roamed their prairie grasslands in millions. But European settlers in North America almost wiped them out by the start of the 20th century, for their meat and hides, and to make way for farm animals. Now the bison have built up numbers again in wildlife parks and wilderness refuges.

374 Ostrich

The ostrich of Africa's savanna grassland holds multiple world records. It's the tallest and heaviest bird, more than 2.5 m high and 140 kg in weight. It's the fastest running bird, and indeed one of the quickest land animals, able to race along at 70 km/h. The female lays the biggest eggs of any bird, each more than 15 cm long and 40 times the size of an ordinary hen's egg. The ostrich also eats an amazing variety of foods, from hard nuts and seeds to worms and lizards.

346 Ruby-throated hummingbird

Only slightly longer than your finger at 9 cm from beak to tail, the ruby-throated hummingbird flies an astonishing 2000 km on its yearly migration. In autumn it travels south from the eastern USA and Canada to spend winter in the Caribbean, Mexico or Central America. It returns the following spring to breed. The red-throated male and white-throated female defend the breeding territory around their nest with fantastic energy, hurling themselves at birds 20 times their size, even predators like hawks and falcons.

383 Cheetah

The cheetah has a body shape more like a greyhound dog than a big cat. Its long, thin legs are one reason for its incredible speed. Another is the way its flexible backbone bends down (as in the photo above) and then up, so that its legs come together and then stretch far apart with each bounding stride. Cheetahs prefer open grassland where they can see far and use their immense speed to chase the fastest prey like hares, antelopes and gazelles.

351 Lion

The so-called 'King of the Beasts', the male lion looks the part with his shaggy mane and huge mouth armed with sharp teeth. However he is not a powerful and deadly hunter. Lions are the only cats to live together, in close groups called prides, and it's the females or lionesses who work together in the hunt. They catch large prey such as zebra, wildebeest and antelopes. The male rarely takes part in finding food. His main tasks are to eat the first and largest helping of the victim, to defend the hunting area or territory of the pride against intruding lions, and to mate with females. When a new lion challenges for pride leadership and wins, he kills any cubs which he has not fathered.

342 Giraffe

The longest legs and longest neck add up to the tallest animal on Earth. The curly, 45-cm tongue means the giraffe can stretch up to 7 m to grasp leaves, buds and fruits. It eats 60 kg of food daily – the weight of an adult person. Giraffes vary in pattern in different regions of Africa. Some are dark brown with thin pale lines; others are 'reversed' with small brown patches on a cream background.

biggest
The male African elephant is the largest land animal, up to 6 tonnes in weight.

fastest
The cheetah runs faster than any other animal, more than 105 km/h.

tallest
The giraffe is the tallest land animal, almost 6 m to the tips of its horns.

For a full key to animals see page 43.

31

Thick coats and non-slip feet

The mountain is one of our harshest environments. Where it is too high, cold and windy for trees to grow, sheltered woods give way to open, rocky scrub. In winter animals face icy winds, driving snow and frozen, slippery ground. In summer the sun shines fiercely through the thin air and rain races away leaving the slopes dry and baked. Thick fur or feathers and strong, agile legs and feet are vital for animals who survive in the mountains.

436 Chough
The alpine chough (pronounced 'chuff') looks like a crow but has a reddish-yellow beak. It hangs around ski resorts and mountain chalets where people feed it with titbits and it scavenges in rubbish. Choughs nest under roofs as well as more naturally on cliffs and crags. Their nesting sites are among the highest of any bird, more than 5500 m up in the Himalayas. The birds fly even higher, over 8000 m, to feed.

471 Apollo butterfly
One of the highest-flying butterflies, the Apollo flaps strongly through the thin air at over 3000 m. It basks on a sunny rock, then feeds on flower nectar. Apollos live from Portugal west to central Asia.

432 Vicuna
The vicuna lives in South America and is the smallest member of the camel family. It is also a rare success of conservation. Its kind were almost wiped out by hunting for meat and fur (a common problem for mountain mammals with thick woolly coats of fine hair). It has been protected by law since 1969 and its numbers have risen to 100,000. Males compete for females by spitting contests.

431 Rock wallaby
Black-footed rocky wallabies hide in caves during the day's intense heat, emerging at dusk to feed. They hop unusually for a kangaroo or wallaby, with the head bent down and the very thick, long, furry

429 Rock hyrax
In ancient Hebrew, grass-eating rock hyraxes were *shaphan*, 'hidden ones'. They disappear like magic among rocks almost before you glance at them. They live in the Middle East and Africa and sweat in an unusual place, on their soles. The slight dampness helps their feet to grip smooth, shiny rocks. A hyrax who strays onto soil takes an hour to clean its clogged-up feet!

tail arched up for balance. The skin on the soles of the back feet is almost scaly for a good grip on boulders and crags. Like other wallabies, rock wallabies are marsupials and the mother rears her young in a pouch. They live in isolated areas of west, central and north-east Australia and eat grass, leaves, fruits, roots, even bark.

439 Snow leopard
Second smallest of the seven big cats (after the clouded leopard), the snow leopard has extremely thick, fluffy fur. It is rare and remote, following prey like small deer up and down the Himalayas with the seasons. Its wide, furry paw-pads cope with both soft snow and hard rocks. The snow leopard stalks a victim until 15–10 m away, then charges with two or three amazing spring-loaded bounds and tears out its throat.

468 Andean condor
This great vulture holds the bird world record for wing area, although it is beaten for wing span (tip to tip length) by the albatross. Its vast silhouette soars over the Andes and spots a dead or dying sheep-sized animal from 5 km away. It can also see another of its kind 10 km away. So as soon as one condor swoops to feed on the carcass, a chain reaction brings another 10 or even 20 condors from hundreds of kilometres around.

448 Snow bunting
The male snow bunting is snow-white in spring except for black bars on his back, tail and wing-ends. In winter he is mottled grey-brown like the female. These buntings nest in the Arctic, farther north than any other small songbird. They breed fast too. The eggs take 12 days to hatch and the chicks leave the nest after only 10 days.

430 Bobcat (bay lynx)
Not much larger than a big pet cat, the bobcat is sturdy, powerful and fierce. It is named after its short, stubby 'bobbed' tail. It preys on rabbits, deermice, squirrels and similar victims, which it stalks through hilly, rocky scrub and also swamps and woods. Bobcats are found in most of North America.

Like many cats the bobcat can spring straight up 2 m or more and slash out with its paws to catch low-flying birds. It is more adaptable than its close cousin the lynx and has coped better with the spread of people and farms. It may take chickens, lambs and even calves. But it preys mainly on wild animals, and porcupine quills have been found in its droppings.

441 Yak
The wild yak of high Central Asia is, with the bison, the biggest of wild cattle. A male yak may be 3 m long, 2 m tall at the shoulder, with horns 100 cm long. It weighs up to 750 kg, as much as 10 large humans. However the female yak is about half this size. Domesticated yak are even smaller. They are kept by local people for their hair, milk, meat and hide (skin).

466 Bighorn sheep
The horns of the ram (male) are 1.2 m around their curve. Females (ewes) have much shorter versions. In the Rockies of North America the rams crash their heads together so hard that they may knock each other out.

highest
Yak survive in Asian ice deserts above 6000 m.

longest
Yak also share the record (with musk oxen) for the longest fur, up to 100 cm.

biggest
The Andean condor is one of the world's most massive flying birds, weighing 11 kg and with wings 3 m across

closest
The little rock hyrax's closest animal cousin is – the huge elephant!

For a full key to animals see page 42.

Ripples, swirls and bubbles

Look into a pond, stream, river or lake. What do you see? Probably a mirror-like reflection of your face! But this is suddenly broken by ripples and bubbles. The surface swirls and you notice shadowy shapes moving beneath. The world of fresh water seems alien to us. But it's home to a teeming variety of fish, frogs, turtles, grubs, worms and other creatures. Many birds also fly or run here to dive beneath the surface and feed.

528 Salmon

Leaping from the water like a dart, the salmon struggles through rapids and up waterfalls as it fights against the river's rushing water. Why? To reach the safe, clear, stony stream where it hatched from an egg five or even 10 years ago. The salmon grew up there and then swam out to sea for a few years. Now it returns to its home stream to breed – and die.

492 Snapper turtle

Turtles lack teeth, but they certainly can bite. The edges of the jaws are made of a sharp horny substance so they work like hard plastic blades. The snapper turtle of North and Central America has one of the strongest bites. It is also fierce and ready to snap at enemies. It could easily snip off your finger. This reptile hunts fish, frogs and worms. It also cracks open and eats shelled animals like crayfish, snails and other turtles.

519 White pelican

The pelican's stretchy chin is its fishing bag. This large water bird scoops its open beak through the water. The throat or gular pouch balloons out as it fills with water and hopefully some fish too or maybe frogs. The pelican then lifts its bill out and tenses the muscles in its pouch to make it smaller. Water pours out but the fish stay put and the pelican swallows its catch. White pelicans are the biggest of the eight types of pelican. They live by lakes and marshes across Southern Europe, Africa and Asia.

552 Leech

Leeches are worms, closely related to the earthworm. They are also parasites. They feed by sucking the blood or body fluids from other animals, called their hosts. Each type of leech specializes in a certain kind of host such as a fish, terrapin or water bird. The leech fastens on with its head sucker and then twists its circular mouth edged with tiny teeth. The mouth works like a cookie-cutter to scrape through the host's skin and into the flesh. The leech can then suck its meal.

478 Beaver

The beaver lives in streams and pools in North America. Its thick fur keeps out chilly wind and water. It can hold its breath and stay underwater for 15 minutes to hide from predators like wolves. Its flat, scaly tail slaps the surface to warn its family of danger. Its sharp front teeth gnaw bark for food and keep growing so they do not wear away. If a beaver never gnawed its teeth would be 2 m long!

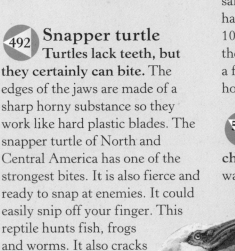

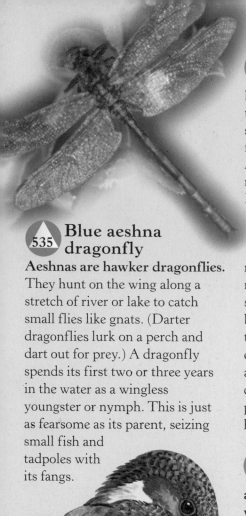

535 Blue aeshna dragonfly

Aeshnas are hawker dragonflies. They hunt on the wing along a stretch of river or lake to catch small flies like gnats. (Darter dragonflies lurk on a perch and dart out for prey.) A dragonfly spends its first two or three years in the water as a wingless youngster or nymph. This is just as fearsome as its parent, seizing small fish and tadpoles with its fangs.

559 Kingfisher

Often the only sign of a kingfisher is a streak of brilliant blue as it flashes along the river bank. It may be flying back to its nest hole with an unlucky fish in its dagger-like beak. The kingfisher catches its prey by diving onto it like an arrow from a bankside shrub or tree. It is usually a shy bird and hides in bushes if people come near.

484 Painted terrapin

Like a brightly painted bath toy, this terrapin paddles through the water with surprising speed. The name 'terrapin' comes from a native American term meaning 'little turtle'. It is used for various small, freshwater members of the turtle group. Like all reptiles, terrapins have lungs and not gills. So they must come to the surface every few minutes to take a breath of fresh air. The painted terrapin chomps with its sharp-edged mouth on small water animals like fish, tadpoles, worms, crayfish and shellfish. For protection it can pull most of its head and legs into its shell.

479 Otter

The otter seems a playful animal, especially when young. It rolls, tumbles and somersaults on the bank and then slips down a mudslide to splash in the water. It looks like fun but it is also serious. The otter is practising for the hunt. It must twist and turn at high speed to swim after and catch its prey, mainly speedy fish.

Eurasian otters are found across Europe, North Africa and Asia. They like quiet rivers and lakes and avoid areas with people. Otters which live near the coast often hunt along the shore for crabs, prawns, shellfish, seabird eggs and chicks.

526 Minnow

The name 'minnow' is sometimes used for any small fish. But the minnow is a distinct kind of fish, although only 10 cm long even when fully grown. Minnows live in groups or shoals and eat tiny prey like baby fish and water fleas.

558 Mute swan

Mute means silent, but this swan is not. It can snort, hiss and even make a feeble version of the trumpeting sound produced by other swans. The mute swan looks peaceful and mild, but again it is not. It snakes out its long neck to peck at smaller birds, flaps its powerful wings at them and chases them away. This is how the cob (male swan) keeps its feeding area clear. It's also how the pen (female) protects the nest and young, called cygnets.

hungriest

A hungry leech can fill its stomach with 10 times its own weight of blood – like you drinking 500 big cartons of tomato juice!

slowest

Swans flap their wings slower than almost any other bird, only once every 2 seconds.

biggest

Dragonfly eyes are the biggest in the insect world. Each one is made of 20,000 tiny units.

For a full key to animals see page 43.

Key to animals

RAINFOREST CANOPY

1 Titi monkey
2 Spider monkey
3 Horned guan
4 Harpy eagle
5 Ornate hawk-eagle
6 Sun conure parrot
7 Asian fairy bluebird
8 Aye-aye
9 Golden-fronted leafbird
10 Golden-throated barbet
11 Giant squirrel
12 Coati (coati-mundi)
13 Crested guan
14 Black-rumped tree frog
15 Flamed minivet
16 Scarlet macaw
17 Hyacinth macaw
18 Blue-and-yellow macaw
19 New Guinea birdwing
   butterfly (x2)
20 Green aracari
21 Yellow-backed sunbird
22 Superb bird of paradise
23 Wilson's bird of paradise
24 Red-headed honeyeater
25 Golden whistler
26 Koala
27 Spectacled flycatcher
28 Swift
29 Red-capped parrot
30 Red-cheeked parrot
31 Palm cockatoo
32 Red-vented parrot
33 Brown capuchin
34 Bearded saki
35 Verreaux's sifaka

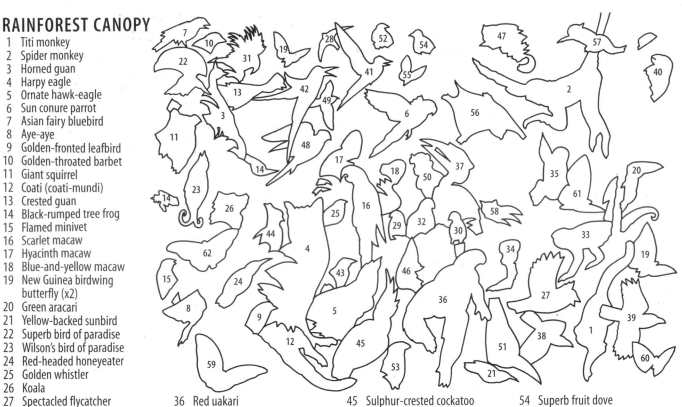

36 Red uakari
37 Great Indian hornbill
38 Multi-coloured barbet
39 Black-collared barbet
40 Green broadbill
41 Rufous-tailed jacamar
42 Paradise jacamar
43 Yellow figbird
44 Topknot pigeon

45 Sulphur-crested cockatoo
46 Turaco
47 Spotted cuscus
48 Collared forest falcon
49 Laughing falcon
50 King vulture
51 Crimson-rumped toucanet
52 Beautiful fruit dove
53 Toucan barbet

54 Superb fruit dove
55 Agrias butterfly
56 Flying lemur (colugo)
57 Red giant squirrel
58 Margay
59 Blue morpho butterfly
60 Davis's chorinea butterfly
61 Goliath birdwing butterfly
62 Indian tree-of-heaven silk moth

JUNGLE FLOOR

131 Okapi
132 Palm civet
133 Jaguar
134 Cassowary
135 Tiger
136 Small-eared dog
137 Malayan tapir
138 Ruby chested pitta
139 Asian elephant
140 Black-headed pitta
141 Peacock
142 Garnet pitta
143 Muntjac
144 Victoria crowned pigeon
145 Common mongoose
146 Great curassow
147 Royal antelope
148 Common piping guan
149 Sambar deer
150 Regent bowerbird (catbird)
151 Wild forest hog
152 Blue-breasted pitta
153 Javan rhinoceros
154 Gaur
155 Moonrat
156 Striped elephant shrew
157 Crested argus pheasant
158 Ringed-tailed lemur
159 Jungle fowl
160 Pangolin
161 Banded pitta
162 Tayra
163 Banded palm civet
164 Spectacled owl
165 Sun bear
166 Forest eagle owl

167 Bongo
168 Central American crested owl
169 Yellow duiker
170 Kagu
171 Sorana butterfly
172 Blue-headed wood dove
173 Mandrill
174 Brown mesites
175 De Brazza's monkey

176 Motmot
177 Leopard
178 Peranthus butterfly
179 Serval
180 Crested francolin
181 Lowland gorilla
182 Thyastes butterfly
183 Ocelot
184 Sardanapalus butterfly

185 Pale-winged trumpeter
186 Hewitson's nessaea butterfly
187 Jabiru stork
188 Drury's antymacnus butterfly
189 Giant anteater
190 Jaguarundi
191 Brocket deer
192 Babirusa (Celebese wild pig)
193 Red-chested pitta

TROPICAL TREES

63 Binturong
64 Greater bushbaby
65 Linsang
66 Green-billed toucan
67 Clouded leopard
68 Long-tailed manakin
69 Tarsier
70 Black-and-white colobus monkey
71 Tree shrew
72 Moustached monkey
73 Slow loris
74 Chimpanzee
75 Orang-utan
76 Channel-billed toucan
77 Lar gibbon
78 White-billed jacamar
79 Golden gecko
80 Emerald tree boa
81 Sloth
82 Cape sugar bird
83 Tamandua (tree anteater)
84 Ross's touraco
85 Kinkajou
86 Blue touraco
87 Howler monkey
88 Elegant trogon
89 White-faced saki
90 Ruby topaz hummingbird
91 Douroucouli (owl or night monkey)
92 Scarlet hummingbird
93 Squirrel monkey

94 Frilled coquette hummingbird
95 Cottontop tamarin
96 Sparkling violet-eared hummingbird
97 Emperor tamarin
98 Diana monkey
99 Red-bellied tamarin
100 Crimson topaz hummingbird
101 Geoffroy's tamarin
102 Blood-red cymothoe butterfly
103 Golden lion tamarin
104 Cuban tody
105 Moustached tamarin
106 Violet sabre-wing hummingbird
107 White uakari
108 Purple-crowned fairy hummingbird
109 Green iguana
110 Long-tailed sylph hummingbird
111 Quetzal
112 Eclectus parrot
113 Keel-billed toucan
114 Red lory
115 Cuvier's toucan
116 Rainbow lorikeet
117 Toco toucan
118 Double-eyed fig parrot

119 Umbrella bird
120 Black-collared love bird
121 Blue-legged tree frog
122 Rhetenor morpho butterfly
123 Columbine tree frog
124 Claudina butterfly

125 Golden tree frog
126 Geoffroy's libythia butterfly
127 Azure tree frog
128 Moon moth
129 Heliconius butterfly
130 Goliath birdwing butterfly

TROPICAL SWAMP

194 Crocodile
195 Allen's swamp monkey
196 Tapir
197 Bichir
198 Rosy-billed pochard
199 Archer fish
200 Indian forest kingfisher
201 Knifefish (notopterus fish)
202 Amazon kingfisher
203 Peter's elephant-snout fish
204 Yellow-billed kingfisher
205 Red-finned black phantom tetra
206 Arapaima (pirarucu)
207 Glowlight tetra
208 Red piranha
209 Pacu
210 Cardinal tetra
211 Capybara
212 Flame tetra
213 Hippopotamus
214 Striped headstander
215 Egyptian goose
216 Golden pencil fish
217 Hammerkop stork
218 Three-striped pencil fish
219 African jacana (lilytrotter)
220 Common hatchetfish
221 White-faced tree duck
222 Red spot tetra
223 African pygmy goose
224 Black ruby barb
225 Black-winged stilt
226 Tinfoil barb
227 Sand plover
228 Red-tailed black shark
229 Pied plover
230 Clown loach

231 Spur-winged lapwing
232 Red aphyo (aphyosemion)
233 Long-toed lapwing
234 Oscar cichlid
235 Blacksmith plover
236 Angelfish
237 Sacred ibis
238 Discus fish
239 Saddlebill stork
240 Four-eyed fish (Anableps fish)
241 Yellow-billed stork
242 Paradise fish
243 African spoonbill
244 Pearl gourami
245 Little bittern
246 Flamingo
247 Night heron
248 Nile monitor
249 Purple heron
250 Malawi golden cichlid
251 Malawi yellow tiger cichlid
252 Malawi green zebra cichlid
253 Malawi blue zebra cichlid
254 Black-spot red gourami
255 Malawi blue cichlid
256 Pelican
257 Purple gallinule
258 Shoebill stork
259 Darter (anhinga or snakebird)
260 Firemouth cichlid
261 Paca
262 Snake-necked terrapin

263 Lechwe (marsh antelope)
264 False gharial (gavial)
265 Amazon river dolphin
266 Brooke's rajah birdwing
267 Electric eel
268 Hottentot teal
269 Red-billed pintail
270 Anaconda
271 Upside-down catfish
272 Botia loach

273 Water opossum
274 Mozambique mouthbrooder
275 Giant otter
276 Scarlet ibis
277 Leopard catfish
278 Matamata turtle
279 Coypu
280 Sitatunga (marsh buck)
281 Red-backed rajah shelduck
282 Arowana

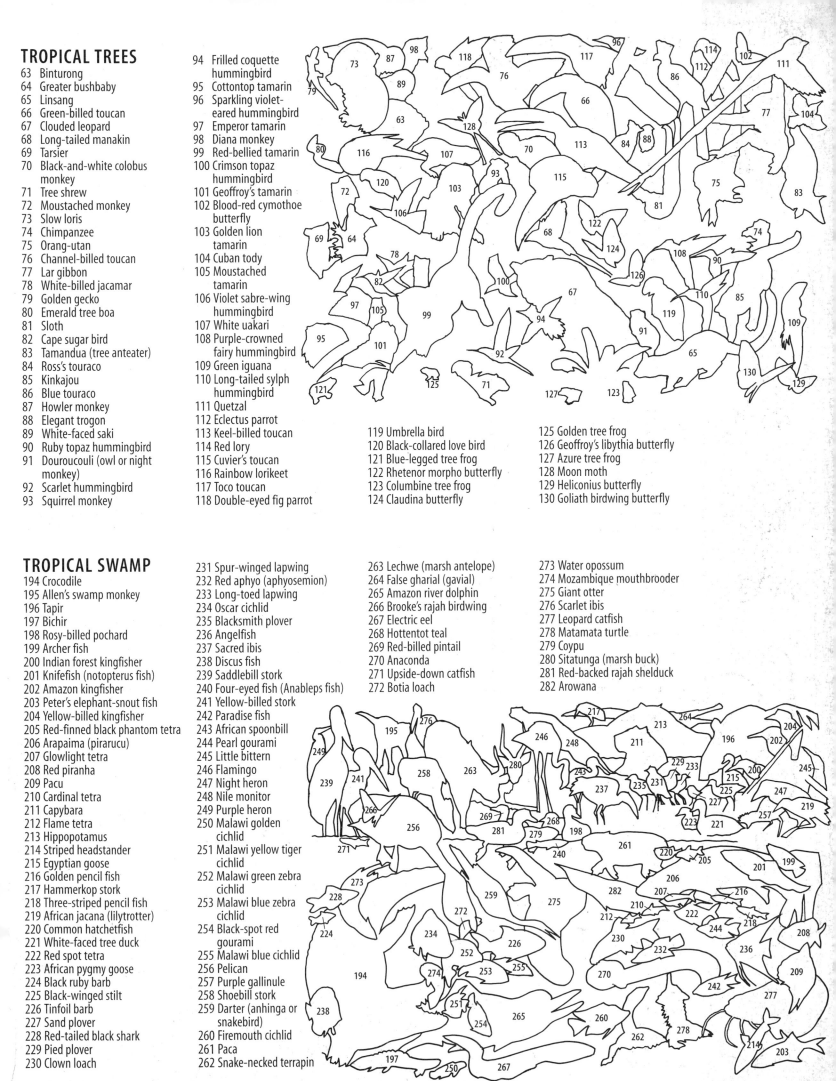

Key to animals

TEMPERATE FOREST

MOUNTAIN AND UPLAND

GRASSLAND AND DESERT

45 Sulphur-crested cockatoo
102 Blood-red cymothoe butterfly
338 Cattle egret
339 European bee-eater
340 Hoopoe
341 Swainson's hawk
342 Giraffe
343 Crowned crane
344 Carmine bee-eater
345 Springhare
346 Ruby-throated hummingbird
347 Cape vulture
348 Marabou stork
349 Yellow-necked spurfowl
350 Masked weaver bird
351 Lion
352 Spotted weaver bird
353 Black rhino
354 Egg-eating snake
355 Kangaroo
356 Gerenuk
357 Citrus (Christmas) swallowtail
    butterfly
358 Wildebeest (gnu)
359 Vulturine guinea fowl
360 Bison
361 Cockatiel
362 Pronghorn
363 Flock pigeon
364 Striped ground squirrel
365 African elephant
366 Meerkat (suricate)
367 Impala
368 Prairie falcon
369 Vervet monkey
370 African monarch (plain tiger)
    butterfly

371 Kudu
372 Whooping crane
373 Grevy's zebra
374 Ostrich
375 Bat-eared fox
376 Warthog
377 Saiga antelope
378 Spotted hyaena
379 Addax antelope
380 Hare
381 Rosy starling
382 Springbok
383 Cheetah
384 Gila monster
385 Lilac-breasted
    roller
386 Two-humped
    (Bactrian) camel
387 Superb starling
388 Burrowing owl
389 Amethyst
    starling
390 Scaled quail
391 Saffron finch
392 Californian quail
393 Painted bunting
394 Roadrunner
395 Red-billed hornbill
396 Guanaco
397 Asian white-backed vulture
398 Maned wolf
399 Water buffalo
400 Sonora blue butterfly
401 Hartebeest
402 Ajax birdwing butterfly
403 Red-cheeked cordon bleu
404 Coyote
405 Melba finch

406 Budgerigar
407 Jackal
408 Galah cockatoo
409 Bishop's weaver bird
410 Firefinch
411 Princess parrot
412 Masked manakin
413 Mitchell's cockatoo
414 Violet-eared waxbill
415 Zebra finch
416 Red-headed finch

417 Painted finch
418 White stork
419 Swallow
420 Jackson's chameleon
421 Paradise whydah
422 Two-banded courser
423 Mourning dove
424 Orange-cheeked waxbill
425 Zebra waxbill
426 Eastern meadowlark

TEMPERATE WETLAND

478 Beaver
479 Otter
480 Coypu
481 Pochard
482 Platypus
483 Tufted duck
484 Painted terrapin
485 Golden-eye
486 Water shrew
487 Red-breasted merganser
488 Spectacled darter
489 Shelduck
490 Pumpkinseed fish
491 Canada goose
492 Snapper turtle
493 Avocet
494 Muskellunge
495 Racoon dog
496 Bream
497 Mink
498 Perch
499 Spoonbill
500 Blue catfish
501 Grey heron
502 Three-spined stickleback
503 Blue-throat
504 Alligator gar
505 North American ruddy duck
506 White bass
507 Smew duck
508 Stippled darter
509 Hooded merganser
510 Pochard (diving)
511 Harlequin duck
512 Carp

513 Mandarin duck
514 Pintail
515 Carolina wood duck
516 Dace
517 Canvas-back duck
518 Mirror carp
519 White pelican
520 Swan mussel
521 Red-necked phalarope
522 Eel
523 Redshank
524 Grayling
525 Curlew
526 Minnow
527 Long-tailed duck
528 Salmon
529 Red-breasted
    goose
530 Great crested newt
531 Black-necked stilt
532 Palmate newt
533 Ram's-horn snail
534 Rainwater
    killifish
535 Blue aeshna
    dragonfly
536 Red shiner
537 Blue damselfly
538 Common shiner
539 Reed bunting
540 Largemouth bass
541 Dabchick
542 Freshwater drum
543 Wilson's phalarope
544 Flying-fox fish
545 Black-tailed godwit

546 Darter fish
547 Common frog
548 Lamprey
549 Bearded tit (reedling)
550 Great diving beetle
551 Large copper butterfly
552 Leech
553 Hellbender

554 River snail
555 Teal
556 Coot
557 Wigeon
558 Mute swan
559 Kingfisher
560 Mallard

Under threat

This book celebrates the beauty and variety of animal life. But some of these creatures are at risk of extinction – dying out altogether. There are numerous reasons why extinction is such a great threat. Sadly, most of them are due to human activities. By far the greatest single threat is habitat loss. This is when people take over wild places and change them into farmland, forest plantations, towns, factories and roads, so the animals have no natural homes. There are many other reasons too, as described below.

154 Gaur

Some animals are naturally rare and probably always have been. Gaur (Indian bison) are wild cattle from the forests of India and Southeast Asia. They prefer small clearings for their favourite food of grassy plants. Such a clearing only forms in the forest when an old tree crashes down leaving a 'hole'. And it soon fills in as new trees grow. So gaur wander from one temporary clearing to another, frequently having to move to a new feeding site. These sites are scattered and scarce, so gaur are too.

325 Hobby

Some creatures have become rare due to human activities, but only in certain areas. The hobby, a small falcon, is a fast and skilful hunter. Many years ago it was common over much of Britain. However it has suffered in various ways. Fewer wild areas means there is less prey to hunt and fewer undisturbed places to nest. Hobbies have also been trapped, poisoned and shot for stuffed bird collections, and their eggs taken by collectors too. Even so, the hobby still lives across much of Europe and spends winter in Africa.

482 Platypus

The huge land mass of Australia has many fascinating animals found nowhere else in the world. These include marsupials or pouched mammals such as kangaroos, wallabies, wombats and koalas, and monotremes or egg-laying mammals such as the platypus. However some Australian creatures at risk from introduced species brought by people. The platypus feeds in water on worms, shellfish and grubs. But it is threatened by introduced pests including rats and certain fish. Also its creeks and billabongs are being drained for surrounding farmland and polluted by chemical fertilizers and pesticides.

505 North American ruddy duck

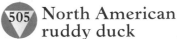

This ruddy duck, as its name suggests, is originally from North America and the Caribbean region. It has been brought to many countries in Europe and Asia as a colourful addition to the waterfowl on lakes and rivers. However the ruddy duck, and other introduced species like the mandarin duck from China, may disturb the balance of bird life. As they take over a lake, they leave less food and fewer nesting sites for the ducks already there. The introduced species are said to 'out-compete' the local ones.

Index